Life Between the Poles

Joe Smith

WALDENHOUSE PUBLISHERS, INC.
WALDEN, TENNESSEE

Life Between the Poles

Type and design by Karen Paul Stone
Published by Waldenhouse Publishers, Inc.
100 Clegg Street, Signal Mountain, Tennessee 37377 USA
423-886-2721 www.waldenhouse.com
Printed in the United States of America
ISBN: 978-1-947589-73-5
Library of Congress Control Number: 2023943482
An anthology of poems written from the viewpoint of a bipolar poet covering topics such as psychotherapy, romance, divorce, whimsy, and the experience of writing poetry itself - Provided by publisher
POE023000 POETRY / Subjects & Themes / General
HEA055000 HEALTH & FITNESS / Mental Health
SEL020010 SELF-HELP / Mood Disorders / Bipolar Disorder

To

my brother
Benedict Jude Smith

FROM THE AUTHOR

This work features an anthology of poems written from the viewpoint of a bipolar poet covering topics such as psychotherapy, romance, divorce, whimsy, and the experience of writing poetry itself.

Contents

Psychotherapy

*It helps to know that bear spray is a repellent and that,
while the polar bear has no land-based predators,
the orca will devour him when he is at sea.*

The BiPolar Bear

I was attacked by a BiPolar Bear
He turned me upside and down
He was last seen wearing a smile
Or maybe he was wearing a frown

His real name is *Ursus Maritimus*
He is a voracious carnivore
He has no natural land predator
His all seal diet I deplore

Attempting to lighten the load
The doctor gave me bear spray
Of many and various kinds
But none quite kept him at bay

There were effects that were long lasting
The attack left me prone to hibernate
I simply mention this in passing
Often thereafter I'd isolate

He comes back again and again
There just is no appeasing him
When he slows down, it seems
The Bear Spray is just teasing him

<u>Joe Smith</u>

His nickname is *Nanook*
And he has only two speeds
3.5 and 25 miles per hour
I can't help but follow his leads

For the faster visits there's remediation
In the form of some kind of salt
Another form of bear medication
Lithium, the 25 mile per hour speed to halt

Ah, the bitter bite of the Bipolar Bear
It happens, it seems, ever more often
With bear spray, lithium, and conversation
The bite of the bear I seek to soften

One thing here should be noted
The bear is a *mourning* person
Thus the bear remains in his lair
In the evening as his feelings worsen

I continue to seek a permanent cure
So as I wiggle, squirm, and flail
I hope and pray to God I can endure
Until he sends me an Orca whale

How It Feels

The dense fog rolls in
Engulfs me and dampens my skin
Blocks out the dim light
Turns an ugly gray day into night

The pills and the prayers cease to work
As I peer inside where the bad spirits lurk
And just as I turn to touch rather than sight
I know for certain that all is not right

So I pack up my fears until the fog clears
And seek to hold on as the end nears
But for my friend it would be the end
A brighter light she continues to send

On Revelation

I pulled the drape and let her see
I fear a bit too much of me
But there's one thing of which I'm certain
I can no longer deny what's behind the curtain

It's no secret that it's best to hide
Most of what we are inside
For once we reveal what there lies
A little part of our person dies

Question # 1

Sent to you for observation
I open up another time
Trying to find some consolation
Without feeling that this is a crime

The question that today you asked me
Is not a thing I have not thought
Do I love her? Yes, completely
I have no fear of getting caught

For I haven't hidden or deceived
The feeling that this process brings
And I have felt somewhat relieved
At this if not in other things

To be with her do I malinger?
Do I string her along?
Do I turn blue so I can see her?
If I did would I be wrong?

Reflection tells me what the fact is
I don't feign the way I feel
Knowing what the final act is
My need of her is very real

Does she have this effect on others?
Do I really want to know?
Her kindness and her presence smothers
My urge to make me finally go

Every day as I leave work
And I go sadly home
To the place where demons lurk
And where the memories roam

I steel myself and so my soul
Which does its best to hide
As I slide back into the hole
And turn all hope aside

So my account is now found factual
No secret to conceal
Both real love and need are actual
At least that's how I feel

Question # 2

What's the point?
Why take the time?
Why hide your thoughts
Enveloped in rhyme?

Have you never sent a letter
To a sorry soul?
Just to make a sad soul better
Seems a worthwhile goal

Again, I ask,
If you've the time
Why force your feelings
Into rhyme?

One more time I will tell you
Why this works so well
I look for answers, not to sell you
To make life less like hell

Tell me now
To whom you send it?
Receipt is proven how?
And how do you know just when to end it?

It needs no address, envelope, or stamp
No postal zone required
It simply has to light my lamp
Then it can be retired

Anxiety

There's something I'd like to explore
In hopes I'll understand it all the more
It's something I always keep with me
Though it keeps me down quite completely

It hides in plain sight most discreetly
And comes out at night most completely
It's fear blown all out of proportion
Despite my most considerable objection

With worry itself in incubation
There comes a need for inoculation
A time for reason to take hold
A time for the psyche to be bold

It flies in the face of intuition
Founded on a base of confused sensation
What's there to fear but fear itself?
Time to wrap up the thoughts, put them on the shelf

A small dose of it is handy, for sure
But blend it with reason don't take it pure
Mix it up with logic they say
You avoid fear, you keep it at bay

But all of this is much easier said than done
When the paranoid thoughts start to run
I give it a try but it's not that I'm able
To harness my thoughts, the discussion to table

I argue and fume, my thoughts to control
Calm sedate thoughts are my only goal
I try not to think but only to pray
And wait out the night until the next day

Joe Smith

Insomnia

Here we go again
Another round to fight
I try to zero in
And get some sleep tonight

But my nemesis awakens me
From an uncertain slumber
The times that he's done this
Are too great to number

He rattles my brain
And opens my eyes
My sleep to disdain
My plan for rest dies

This is another night
Like so many others
He'll put up a fight
He'll get his druthers

I'm almost afraid
To go to my bed
This plan that he's laid
Gets into my head

The thoughts come so fast
They send my head reeling
Both future and past
Parsed with a paranoid feeling

Mistakes made in the past
Are his favorite fodder
He makes sure they last
Calls court to order

Judgments he'll pass
There will be no defense
No peace at last
No forgiven offense

Here I sit all alone
No one beside me
No one to phone
No cloak to hide me

Must deal with him solely
As he sits on the bench
No matter how lowly
My heart to wrench

Joe Smith

What Are The Odds

I have this sinking feeling
Each time I stop to think
You've left my weak mind reeling
Caused my broken heart to sink

To dare to break a confidence
Would lead me to the brink
It's more than mere coincidence
This maddening marriage link

If you had never sent me
To that therapeutic group
I never would have heard of him
Or been drawn into the loop

But you did send me there
And there I went
And that place is where
I saw his armor's dent

Yes it's true I never met him
But if her story I'd deny
Then all else I found within
Would have to be a lie

Oath dictates I not tell you
And I won't break that trust
But it's killing me to sell you
A dream soon to turn to dust

He's not the right man for you
Of that I'm certainly sure
But my promises I assure you
Will by right surely endure

If I had never heard of him
Or if I had not met you
The chance of both is so slim
Now I fear that he will get you

> You promised me you'd never tell
> All the things I've told to you
> Now I'm dying in a living hell
> 'Cause I made a promise too

Joe Smith

Another Visit

I walk into the room and sit in the chair
Half the time wondering why I came there
I open my mouth and say all that I dare

It's a one sided, structured, official affair
Sometimes seems selfish I'm the only one there
Who does any talking, no notes to compare

You say the relationship is something real
So why is it only lonely I feel?
Still without you there's no hope that I'll heal

Your grace in the face of whatever disaster
Tells me there is nothing that you cannot master
You dress up my wounds in new confidence plaster

But why is it I still feel so upended
And fear the thing has already ended
Except for the footnotes to be appended
And my constant fear that I have offended

There's nothing outside of my problems we share
Yet I delude myself into thinking there's something there
That will last so much longer than the time that we share

My days have all changed and that's quite a feat
No problem comes that I don't share with you complete
At times there is no need to repeat
What's already been said, though we didn't meet

Midnight Mystery Matinee

Now I lay me down to sleep
I pray I'll find no trouble deep
No demons, I hope, are lurking there
No labyrinth there to me ensnare

The marque is blank, no hint of despair
No clue as to what pitfalls are there
No cast of characters can be found
The show begins without any sound

As I enter into this night's haze
I hope to escape from any maze
That tries to trap me in its webs
I'd free myself 'fore my energy ebbs

I slowly move across the void
Unpleasant thoughts I try to avoid
Sleep comes, it seems, slowly but surely
Rest comes with risk, not respite purely

Confidence broken is a frequent subject
Psychic distress is a common effect
Secrets, it seems, told for all to hear
Releasing them now is my greatest fear

And what of the monsters that make an appearance?
Can I make them leave me alone without interference?
Dragons and vampires appear in the mist
When morning comes I hope they won't persist

I wait in my bed for the intermission
Protective heroes I seek to commission
Vacant theater seats around me abound
No scripted help for me can be found

And darkness itself can be quite a chore
Light brings me relief and so much more
When mad dogs and jackals appear on the screen
It's light alone that drives them from the scene

Joe Smith

My British Friend

She held her anger in her teeth
A result of the pain that bit beneath
The scar she wore upon her arm
The outward sign of all the harm
That made her think she'd lost it all
While the rest of us sat there agape and in awe

I've never seen a woman like this
Before she left she gave me a kiss
A moment forever frozen in time
A gift I will savor forever; it's mine
The events of my life I often sift
And of all in my screen I savor this gift

No one I've met, or will I think
Could disarm me with a single wink
Exotic beauty beyond compare
I couldn't believe I found myself there
Despite my appearance and my condition
She took the time, she paid attention

When Reality Gets Bent

I'm sometimes given to hallucination
When reality takes a short vacation
When objects in the mirror aren't as they appear
And the sounds that come at me aren't all that I hear

Voices in the attic
Promote psychic static
Specters descend down the stairs
Catching me unawares

Invaders that depart without opening the door
Lend not a clue that there can be no more
Famous bodies and faces show up in places
Highly unlikely as the moon goes through its phases

Court was held among all those strangers
Believing it real constituted the dangers
Thinking truly, I'd just been dismissed
By a phantom agent whose help I'd enlist

Calling for help seemed somehow futile
The authorities came and the response was quite brutal
They were no help, yes no help at all
They only made me regret making the call

Somewhat more real but no less disconcerting
The delusions come with uncertainty lurking
Reason alone provides no relief
As I'm certain and sure of my false belief

No one believes me of that I'm sure
But I am convinced, my motives pure
Confirmation of my thoughts simply surrounds me
That they can't be true simply astounds me

Messages are sent me by radio waves
No peace provided that my mind craves
Only support for my false belief
No reasonable thought to provide some relief

So what to do in the future when reality's bent
And I wonder where my sanity went
When the thoughts that I'm thinking drive me up the wall
And I can't seem to find my way through it all

When flashes of truth get all distorted
And facts not quite true are by me reported
When feelings upset me and cause me to panic
And cause my demeanor to veer towards the frantic

I guess I'll stay quiet, raise no alarm
And absorb all the facts that are causing me harm
Keep to myself and maintain the peace
And hope that the panic doesn't increase

The Visit and The Wait

Searching for life's sunny tropics
Passage paid by psychotropics
Living with these soul myopics
I last another day

To your office, I come to visit
Wondering just how fair is it
I'd make it so if I could wish it
I wish it were that way

Muddling through the maddening mist
Armed each time with my wish list
The obvious I won't have guessed
When I go home today

And even if I'm sure I know
Just what you mean I cannot show
My mind will not let it be so
There's nothing left to say

I wait two weeks and bear the pain
I know quite well I'll come again
Certain that I'm not quite sane
And then I go away

For just about a half a minute
I feel my life without me in it
The battle's lost I cannot win it
Can't keep the dog at bay

To be part of something grand
To have and hold it in my hand
Then let it slip away like sand
As my days slip away

I wonder if there'll ever be
A place of mine for me to be
A place with some security
If only for one day

Trying not to be oblique
I give these lines another tweak
It's something more than truth I seek
My thoughts get in the way

And even though I'm sure I know
Just what it takes to make it so
I just can't seem to let it go
I don't know what to say

If I could I'd let you see
The part of me I cannot free
I'd finally drift on out to sea
But I get in my way

My head won't even let me be
When I find my serenity
Because I can't let me be me
It's far too much to pay

So here I sit and hold the bit
Trying to make sense of it
Although it matters not a wit
I try to let me stay

And if I finally take a stand
Erase the fear, strike up the band
Try to live as if life's grand
I'll finally fade away

So what it means, I know you know
Because three times you've told me so
And I know there's no place to go
And still no place to stay

Hidden by this woven veil
My efforts all will surely fail
Whenever my ship starts to sail
I get in my own way

I tie myself before the mast
And do my best to face the past
In hope's I'll see myself at last
Before I rot away

Sometimes my thoughts grow grandiose
My nouns and verbs veer toward verbose
That's when I hate myself the most
Yet still I go my way

Everything that comes to mind
Goes through a filter, charcoal lined
Just so I avoid a bind
To keep the pain away

For so very long I had the music
Now every day I seem to lose it
Face to face I'd rather chose it
Memories block the way

The things she said got me excited
But I won't go where uninvited
The thoughts I have won't get me knighted
I have no right to stay

I write this now as if you'd read it
You don't need but I do need it
And it's for my sake that I plead it
The hope for one fine day

A day when I feel fit
If only for the thought of it
A day when my mind's light is lit
So I'll avoid decay

Late at night as I try to sleep
I cling to memories I'd like to keep
But they sink ever further into the deep
I lose them as I lay

So I spend all my time trying to rekindle
The feelings I have wrapped around my life's spindle
Neither black nor white, but rather a brindle
Separating curds from whey

I sit and spin my talisman
I wish I weren't a shallow man
Although I'm doing all I can
With thoughts I can convey

You sit there in your chair and wait
For me to figure out my fate
To free myself from all this weight
I wish it were today

Seeking Asylum

Sometimes I go away for a while
Sometimes it has been in style
Other times it wasn't so quaint
Wound up with eaters of paint

One time I went to the desert
My misery there to assert
One time I went to Topeka
In hopes of a Psycho Eureka

In Topeka the rooms were all private
The Staff was proud of the quiet
My needs there were very acute
Thankfully the doctors astute

In addition to gaining perspective
Through exercises reflective
I met some people there
For whom I continue to care

No real names can I reveal
So I'll choose some with appeal
The first one I will call Sue
But any other name would due

Sue married her father figure
Marital bliss and a home to configure
But her husband lost interest in her
Alas, he wasn't a winner

You can see that Sue was quite sad
The situation was driving her mad
She came to Topeka to seek some relief
At least that was my humble belief

But Sue had a plan of action
She sought little more than distraction
The sessions had little effect
She simply suffered affection neglect

Sue had a little blue convertible
From which the wheat fields were more discernible
We'd watch the spikes shift in the wind
I prayed it never would end

Later in the desert I met Judy
She was truly a beauty
At the end of each morning meeting
She'd give me a hug as a greeting

Judy was a stage seven alcoholic
She was also somewhat melancholic
Somehow, though, she always made me smile
I would often sit with her for awhile

We kept in touch after the desert
I prayed she would not get hurt
But despite how hard I tried
Soon after we met, Judy died

My desert work was all undone
Her sudden death did me so stun
I've tried but never gotten over it
Though I've tried my best to shoulder it

More recently I sought refuge
From some of life's daily deluge
In institutions more domestic
Though I was quite pessimistic

The facilities were somewhat lacking
In programs and patient tracking
With two to five people per room
Arrangements didn't dispel the gloom

One time I had a roommate
I found out about him too late
He just couldn't stop talking
I spent most nights just walking

I met no one there who could compare
With Judy so fair or Sue I declare
No one I could really care for
No one I could be there for

So if there's need of future institutionalization
I'm looking for a new location
One without the memories
Impinging on the remedies

Joe Smith

Keep It to Myself

It's time that I wrote you to say how I feel
Now that you've gone and done it my nightmare is real
If you could have married a man that I didn't know
I might have accepted and let sorrow grow

Until it expanded throughout my whole being
And dropped me down further, but still left me breathing
This situation is too strange to contemplate
There's too much within to which I relate

I fear that you've gone and made a mortal mistake
Though there's nothing to do, no steps I can take
It's none of my business, be certain I know
But, I can't help the feeling that continues to grow

Yes you're my savior, of that have no doubt
Know, though, that's not what I'm talking about
Over the years through glimpses I've seen
I've grown to love you; you've made you my queen

You've warned me enough not to idolize
But, the one that rises from falls is the one that I prize
Please take a moment and tell me if you see
Something within me that you'd want to be

To recognize a feeling, a thought, or worthy trait
In someone else is to approach heaven's gate
And if there's a way to find the right key
You open your heart and set yourself free

All that aside, I am wondering now
If I would have told you if not for my vow
You've promised to keep all my thoughts secret
But if you spoke to save me I'd have no regret

What I was told in confidence tight
Needs, I believe, to be showered in light
To save you from heartache only seems right
And not to tell you about him takes all my might.

Joe Smith

The Commencement

My name is Joe and I'm bipolar
And tonight I feel grateful, but sad
But when I look out and see all of you
I can't help feeling sort of glad

I came to the desert because life was uncertain
I felt I had no reason to live
But the friends I met here and that I hold so dear
Made me realize I had something to give

Before I left home, I was truly alone
I no longer felt: I was numb
I sped down the street my life to complete
Many things that I did were just dumb

My first day here I felt just like hell
But He sent me friends from room eleven
And on my day worst when I thought I would burst
I met the first of these angels from heaven

On those days that I thought I'd go mad
He found a way to make me serene
By turns He would send the spirits to move me
Of Julie, Lynn, Kelly, and finally Francine

There was more help waiting for me in a group
Where mere chance selection never would do
No the composition was very specific
Including Chuck, Myra, Doug and Malu

There were long talks with many of my roommates
Like Jack, Jim , and Mark, and of course Chuck
And if you can't get a laugh out of that group
Then for sure, you're just out of luck

And then there are others who touched me
In a very special or odd sort of way
Like Andy who learned the secret handshake
And Tallulah who I loved to hear sing and to play

And, of course, I can't forget Catherine
Who taught me to ask for that which I need
And Amy and Sara and Gilbert and Cecilia
My love for you all makes my heart bleed

New friends arrived every day
Like fresh loaves of bread on the baker's shelf
There were Pierce, Sylvia, Fritz, Mike and Mark
I love you all, I can't help myself

But now it's time for me to go
To make room for others to mend
But I want to make sure you know
Each of you will be, forever, my true friend

<u>Joe Smith</u>

ML

I need to write a letter
So I'll write this one to you
It's not that there's anyone better
Or anyone else that would do

If there's nothing else I've learned
In coming to you all these years
It's that I've never been burned
For letting you know all my fears

I know that you must think it stupid
For me to think this way at all
But at least you'll let me say it
And not force me to grovel and crawl

Though there's no chance that I'll ever know you
The way that you've been subjected to me
It's simply one more "have to"
That constantly eats into me

I told you once that I didn't know
Exactly what love is supposed to be
When I'm at my worst and feeling so low
Me, myself, and I seem to agree

But the truth of this matter is nearer
To my understanding than I'll ever admit
As it comes into view so much clearer
To the truth I must finally submit

Fear or Wish?

The end I fear
Is very near
Time to settle accounts
In whatever amounts
The time to pay my life's wages
The time to read my life's pages

For all this time I've walked this earth
For all this time I've felt no worth
The wish to die has been pervasive
Now death's near, it feels invasive
How will I justify the waste
That I have been in my life's haste

How now can I justify
The life I've led with the wish to die
Now that the signs of death appear
I reflect on thoughts full wrought with fear
I see the marks of my death creeping
May it come while I am sleeping

I've never been able to figure out
The black outlook I've been about
Is it just me or are others near
To whom their painful life is dear
Where was the thought to make the most?
Where are the deeds of which to boast?

<u>Joe Smith</u>

Neurotic Ramblings on Transference

The feeling's strong
A kind of longing
A simple song
Of not belonging
Fills me full
Each time I call
I feel a pull
Throughout my all
I can't explain
Just what it means
A numbing pain
Is how it seems
A need to hold
And to be held
A feeling bold
A need to meld
To finally feel
I passed the test
To feel I'm real
Just like the rest
At times I wander
Nowhere to go
I sit and ponder
I need to know
Have I traded
Fear for illusion
Friendships faded
Into delusion

Or something more
That cannot be
I let love's lore
Make a fool of me
Your presence warms me
I sit by your fire
Here nothing harms me
It's a strong desire
To be truly cared for
While wanting to care
What is this endured for
And why can't I share
Secret thoughts that cure
In mysterious ways
I just can't endure
While I'm in this haze
Sitting on the other side
My sight is gone
And then I hide
I simply look
The other way
'Cause something took
My soul away
I hide by staring
At the floor
Continually caring
And wanting more
It makes me feel

More lonely, see
When I turn off what's real
And turn to fantasy
Believe me I know
How this must appear
If you asked me to go
I'd realize my fear
Why can't I just
Let this love go
Why is it I must
Make sure you know
It may not seem
At all logical
Sometimes I think
It's pathological
How did I get
Me into this mess
It's a safe bet
That I'll never guess
No matter how much
I would protest
You'd prove to me such
Is left alone best
It's a part of the process
No need to remind me
Part and parcel of progress
That I leave it behind me
When I finally reach
The end of the road
Then will we each
Lay down the load

For you there'll be
Another file
But as for me
I'll miss your smile
I know that I
Will have to leave
Another "Good Bye"
A new reason to grieve
But you've taught me well
In our Friday sessions
The truth to tell
Some were confessions
And so I confess
And I apologize
But I can't love you less
That, too, I realize

Romance

Joe Smith

The Feel of One Hand Holding

We spent the time alone together
Closer I hoped we'd become
A mutual affection I hoped we'd un-tether
And we'd both feel less a solitary one

I reached out in every way I could
I hoped she would finally understand
I feared that it would do no good
Our footprints would be lost in the sand

There were brief moments of connection
Despite the fence she had erected
And with my best powers of detection
A smile in her eyes I detected

We spent two whole days in a search
For a new home where she could grow
I had no plans of leaving her in the lurch
And that is what I waited for her to know

Despite the fear she has of me
Despite her frightened quake
I hoped she would know how good it would be
If she came to know me for her own sake

What's the Connection?

I drove south for a short vacation
In search of something other than recreation
Although I had no maps or plans
An unknown force drove me to warm southern sands

A short call placed to a time long ago
A machine answers, I told you so
Leave a message at the beep
On impulse I did, now I can't sleep

Showered and dressed and ready to go
I call again hoping she won't say, "No"
In the wrong place, I fear her rejection
Instead I am asked, "What's the connection"

Feeling no right to say, I started to stammer
The blood at my temples started to hammer

A lump in my throat, I swallowed my words
My heart began to race like a hummingbird's
Knowing full well what I'd like to say
I hold it in so she won't run away

A place we can meet is finally chosen
In Florida nothing can stay too long frozen
As my eyes meet hers, she starts to warm
I whisper a prayer that she comes to no harm

For I know she suffers a propensity
For addictions and self-harming activity
And if there was a way I could protect her
Forever I would and never neglect her

So long ago she treated me kindly
A beautiful woman she smiled at me blindly
I'm sure of this now for if she could see
I know she could never be so nice to me

"Anything you could want, what would you wish for?"
"Ask me straight out, what do you fish for?"
"I just want you to see what would make life worthwhile".
"Then that would be you", I said without guile

"How can you say that, you don't even know me".
"After twenty odd years, now how can that be?"
"It's only an image you've grown in your mind".
"I'm telling the truth, not just trying to be kind".

"How do you know? This is infatuation!"
"With all due respect, that's your interpretation".
"I still don't understand, what's the connection?"
"If I understood, I'd cure this infection".

But to this day I haven't a clue
As to what it is that I should do
What if she's right and I don't know my mind
Well, I could do worse than find someone so kind

At Her Request

She asked me if I'd take the time
To express what I thought enveloped in rhyme
Although this could be a big mistake
It's just a chance I'll have to take

She knows the color of her eyes
Is the one I choose to visualize
The one I always contemplate
Each time I try to meditate

Sometimes she'll even use a hug
To lift me from this hole I've dug
When floundering in my deep depression
She cares, I think, at least that's my impression

I'll never forget that unexpected impression
Her lips on my cheek, my heart skipped a compression
I know it meant nothing to her at the time
But for me it was different, that kiss won't leave my mind

And when I recover, for recover I must
For the hope that I feel will soon turn to dust
But until then there's one thing I'd like to say
I hope that kiss comes back home some day

The effect that she has on so many like me
Is to give us a moment of wanting to be
Understood only by those who've fought off the dog
For a few brief moments she's a memory to log

Could things have been different somehow
If they weren't as they are, as we find them now
I know this makes no sense, no sense in the least
But I know her presence beats back the beast

Though I know no feeling if I don't feel guilt
The dense dark jungle between us begins to wilt
And for just one moment, one moment I know
That the friendship between us begins to grow

There can be no doubt, we don't always agree
That's the best part, she's she and I'm me
No effort wasted forcing minds into molds
What each one believes, each one of us holds

End of the Line

"Excuse me", I said, "for making this call"
To the recording that answered, casting a pall
On my hope for some contact with someone there
Someone who knows me and knows that I care

She left me without leaving a clue or a note
As if it were winter and I had no coat
Walked away from me now and it doesn't seem fair
Packed up and moved on as if she didn't care

So I spend all my time on the telephone line
Hoping for answers and wasting my time
You can't get an answer from someone's voice mail
So I look up to heaven, I curse, and I wail

If I have to spend all my time here alone
Why did she give me this number to phone?
What did I do, not do, or say
To make her feel she had to treat me this way?

She called me last as I climbed out of hell
Talked to me sweetly and made my heart swell
So what has happened to this friend of mine?
Why can't I reach her on her private line?

It's Going to be Alright

She asked me if I danced at all
"No, not in a long long time"
She said,"Let's try it you won't fall"
I said, "alright, that's fine."

All evening I had wished I could
Ask her or be struck blind
I never thought that she would do
Just what was on my mind

I prayed that she would ask me to
(I couldn't, 'cause I can't dance)
I didn't know what I would do
Now she was giving me a chance

So long it's been since I've been close
To anyone at all
And here I got a double dose
Though I nearly lost the call

She could have asked me anything
And I would have said, "Yes"
Her soft smooth, soothing voice must sing
To birds and angels is my guess

All night I saw behind her eyes
What she had just been through
Her best attempts could not disguise
Her pain, and sorrow too

But in spite of all that's hurting her
She's made me feel at ease
If I could change the things that were
It's a chance I'd gladly seize

My heart was pounding out a beat
As we walked onto the floor
And even with my two left feet
I could want for nothing more

The softness of her sweet perfume
Was proof of her refinement
I gazed out at the spinning room
And prayed for my confinement

And when she reached out for my hand
To lead me to an open space
Up closer, near the blaring band
My mind began to race

What if I made a fool of me?
The anxiety I feared
Then she stopped and smiled at me
The others disappeared

She draped her arms around my neck
I prayed they never would unwind
I sighed and thought, "Oh what the heck"
She's beautiful and kind

We swayed and stepped and spun around
As lost youth came to pay a call
Bittersweet memories did abound
Thus steeled I was certain not to fall

I did my best to imitate
All of those around me
What I could not initiate
Had now reached out and found me

I felt the softness of her cheek
Pressed smooth against my ear
And though my knees were getting weak
Stumbling was no longer my great fear

For what I felt upon my feet
Was light, too light to fall
But then my heart skipped a beat
And I clearly saw it all

No, clumsy stumbling was not the fear
That I was finally facing up to
But my heart was so scarred by someone close
What was I falling into?

She didn't have to be so kind
No, she didn't have to do it
Now I don't wish to be struck blind
Even though there's nothing to it

To her it was as nothing
That I realized
But for me it was a magic thing
A memory crystallized

I can't help the way I feel
But I could ask for nothing more
Than to have had one dance
And to have had a chance
To have known her a little more

Writing

Magic Mental Medicine

Poetry's one of the healing arts
It helps to write when your heart smarts
There are many ingredients in this pill
All selected to cure your ills
Experts say you should refrain
From over use of the quatrain
And so I'll simply stack these lines
And see if thereby the meaning shines
To write right well brings some relief
At least that is my true belief
A little bit of alliteration
Tends to lighten a bad situation
Rhyme and rhythm are vaccination
Encapsulating that same situation
Symbolism is another tool
As long as you don't break a rule
Metaphor and simile
Can help your reader see
Just what you mean within your text
When your poor mind is vexed
A tiny touch of imagery
Can warm the soul, set you free
You can get a bang out of onomatopoeia
The sounds of which can tend to free ya'
Curious how consonance adds to the cadence
While holding anxiety in abeyance
Sometimes the chemistry includes allusion

Where thoughts and words are in collusion
And "Oh dear chemist I can see!"
When added in is apostrophe
And then there's always irony
As when the blind refuse to see
Sometimes the chemist adds a pun
A tale about a tail is fun
And of course there's repetition
It bears repeating in the preparation
Is all this a formula for mental medication?
Is part and parcel of a rhetorical formation.
In all there are so many ways
To help us through our dismal daze
I hope this wasn't a bore
Despite my mixed metaphor

Joe Smith

The Teacher's Pet

Whenever I try to make me see
I lapse into a simile
To understand a little more
I call upon the metaphor

The teacher in anticipation
Of the student's graduation
Seeks for clearer conversation
And avoids equivocation

Something seemingly incomprehensible
Proves to be quite conventional
When described in terms somewhat whimsical
Clothed in garments understandable

"The darkness was like a big black ball"
Seems sometimes to describe it all
But to say, "it is a lump of coal"
Strikes much nearer to the goal

The cold can be said to "be like ice"
But to increase comprehension twice
Call the cold "a dead man's hand"
And make the simile seem bland

In an effort to knock down the door
To the hall of what we'd know much more
There's no need to implore
Use the magic metaphor

Metaphor #2

I've always strained the metaphor
And now before I strain one more
There's a thing I'd like for you to do
Please listen now until I'm through

In an effort to make you understand
Facts as I see them here at hand
I'll describe the odd in a way that's clear
To me and not to you I fear

With a passion born of sheer emotion
I concoct a cockeyed verbal potion
To lead you to an understanding
Poor verbal talent notwithstanding

Be patient now I beg of thee
As I try to set my feelings free
A leaf on the wind or wave on the ocean
I stretch the fabric of my notion

And after all is said and done
I regret the possible harm I've done
To all the things we never had
Because my choice of words is bad

So many things I'd have you know
Like the way, over time, my love would grow
But for lack of means to tie words together
The weight of my love must seem a feather

And now our time together expires
I realize the effort true love requires
Not only in terms of devotion and time
But also in terms of illusion and rhyme

To say what I feel is more than a chore
Than anything I've done heretofore
And my frustration with all this makes me think
That I'd have fared better with paper and ink

My Futile Attempts

I don't know why I struggle so
Should just give in and let it go
Some words to link and some to show
Some to forget and some just to know

My target group doesn't share my passion
For words all arranged in this final fashion
It makes me feel like I've wasted my time
Assembling words that happen to rhyme

I've saved all these up for quite awhile
Constructed them one at a time without guile
But nobody seems to want them I fear
I've wasted my time so it would appear

But in building them up I've had some relief
From the black dog, the accompanying grief
It's helped to occupy my mind don't you see
And let the anxiety drain out of me

Today's Effort

Now is the time
To write down in rhyme
The thoughts as they come
Before they're undone

It may take some effort
To write something clever
I just sit and stare
And hope something's there

It's art that I'm craving
I hope it's worth saving
I write if I dare
I hope with some flair

Today I'm not manic
But still prone to panic
The ideas are slow
Still I'll give it a go

I could write that I'm lonely
But that surely would only
Show that I'm selfish
And this effort is rubbish

So I'll broaden my outlook
New ideas I'll now brook
I'll search all around me
For something I can't see

Well, I made good on my effort
But found nothing clever
To share with you today
So, there's no need to pay

Joe Smith

Starting Over

It's been a long time
Since I've tried my hand at rhyme
Eight years or more
But my psyche's getting sore

It's no longer automatic
But it's somewhat autocratic
Demanding of my time
But hiding all the rhyme

It used to be so simple
And so very elemental
But now it's more a chore
Trying not to be a bore

I told her I would try it
Not quite sure that she would buy it
But I cannot help but try it
If it will make this mad mind quiet

What else is there to do
When the mood it turns so blue
Why do I even care?
I get some comfort there

It serves as a distraction
And there is some satisfaction
In the laying of the lines
In search of better times

Sometimes the words come to me
But not any words will do me
They must be chosen with care
To leave some meaning there

And should I be distracted
From the lines I first enacted
I can always start again
Newer thoughts come rushing in

And when the mood is fast
As it has been in the past
I give myself a break
If only for sanity's sake

Just An Exercise

I don't know what to say
I feel all dried up today
It doesn't matter anyway
No serious matter left to weigh

They say if you want to write
Something worth reading
You should write every day
Even if you've nothing to say

Today I feel all dried up
My feelings I fear are tied up
I'm still waiting to see
If the drug changes me

It's obvious my heart isn't in it
If this were a race, I wouldn't win it
Nothing of import to share
No reason to read it, and none to care

Joe Smith

A New Piece

Praying now for inspiration
Passage paid by perspiration
Seeking now the perfect word
That 'til now has not been heard

Trying to make the pieces fit
I try to make some sense of it
Some verbal combo that shines
Sweating as I lay these lines

Trying not to force the rhyme
I'll get there yet, just give me time
I scratch my head and walk about
To try and get the feeling out

Sometimes the work will please me
Other times it can't appease me
I only know I can only try
In hopes it will release me

By writing down the words I find
I settle down the monkey mind
Relief it comes but it is fleeting
Sometimes it seems it's self-defeating

Divorce and Aftermath

Joe Smith

Used Up

They all said she'd never leave
Her comfort was too dear
Now her plan it seems was to deceive
She fooled us all I fear

I've known her for over thirty years
At least I thought I knew her
Now I wait as the dusty air clears
I think I can see right through her

So many times she found the need
To bother to accuse me
When all the while she sowed the seed
To grow new ways to use me

Delta

The storm clouds have been brewing
For twenty years and more
And I've been floating aimlessly by
Beyond the sight of shore

The clouds blocked out the sunshine
But 'til now also the pain
It was alright 'til she crossed the line
Now I'm on my own again

When I stood there bound before the mast
In the cold and driving rain
I was staring right into my past
Still I stayed and took the blame

But recently I found a change
When I stop to take it in
To be that mean's beyond my range
So I'll take it on the chin

I don't know what the future holds
Or how this will all work out
If pain and time a character molds
Then it's time for breaking out

I wonder how I'll live alone
What's the chance that I can take it
It doesn't seem so overblown
To think that I won't make it

True I've lived alone before you see
Back when I was a child
With all those people close to me
A fact I've never reconciled

A friend of mine explained to me
The irony of the situation
And she never once complained to me
About my failure to make the connection

It isn't like I had no doubts
She was right in her analysis
It's only with the ins and outs
I'm prone to prefer paralysis

So after it's all over and I'm on my own
I'll try to make some connection
But this time I hope I won't be alone
When it comes time for re selection

Motion to Dismiss

Meet me at the courthouse at nine
I'll really let my selfishness shine
And I'll be mean for meanness's sake
I'll make as much fuss as one cuss can make

I'll do all in my power to make you feel small
To make you feel squeamish, to make your skin crawl
I'll raise up your pride on the tip of my lance
Your soul will feel the soles of my feet as I dance

Just as I've trampled you all these years
I'll trample again to the gallery's cheers
Just as my brand of justice served me in the past
It will serve me again, your strength won't last

And little by little I'll make you feel small
'Til you feel nothing more than a fly on the wall
And when you rise up to take your leave of my sight
I'll knock you back down with all of my might

As you glance, side to side, seeking escape
I'll pillage your ego, your psyche I'll rape
And just to remind you of all gone before
I'll read out our history with my back to the door

While you twist and turn and seek some relief
I'll trample with vengeance on your every belief
I'll gouge out your eyes and fill their sockets with doubt
And do all these things before letting you out

And the funniest thing, the funniest by far
Is you let me do all of this, none will you bar
Because you can't see me as others seem to see
You only see me the way you want me to be

So I take advantage and even the score
In a game you never played which I'll play evermore
And from pillar to post I'll blindly lead you
Until you're dead, I'll fully bleed you

Joining the Dance

In all there were the five of us
Three women and two men
All leaving unions in the dust
Trying to start our lives again

There's the one that I call Jet
Black hair, dark eyes and a devilish grin
While she's as bold as a woman can get
She's our fresh air blowing in

She voices her displeasure
At her former favorite friend
And she gives him full measure
Sure he'll get his in the end

And then there's the Latin Lover
A small precious child in my eye
She dances and then runs for cover
'Cause the slow songs make her cry

I worry about her often
Even though I barely know her
All the hard hearts she could soften
She needs no one to show her

Next there's the dancing fool
His constant genuine grin
He simply can't sit down
He makes the festivities begin

Joe Smith

You cannot help but like him
Almost everybody does
The rest get sucked in by his grin
How's he do all the things he does?

And then there's our newest friend
Blonde hair, bright eyes and model thin
She's sweet and kind, a one of a kind
All our heart's she'll surely win

I know there's something about this Dream
About this, our most recent acquisition
Now that she is on the scene
She can play in most any position

Over the years the group will fade
Each one will go his way
But the fond friendships that we made
Time will never steal away

Today I couldn't find
The Latin Lover or the Dream
But they remain upon my mind
As if they were on the scene

I hope to see them all some day
Safe from their "might have beens"
But until then they all will stay
Within my camera's lens

Tonight

I decided not to go tonight
What I'm feeling isn't fright
But what it is, is just as real
Another form of fear I feel

No it isn't just that I'm alone
Or that I've lost my hard won home
It's simply that among my friends
The loneliness no longer ends

I feel a ghost among their lives
A wasted soul that hell connives
To burn forever and for all ways
Promising sleep, no more painful days

I promised Her that I would fight
The constant urge to take the flight
To fly away from hell on earth
And to see what this life is worth

The last two years we lived in strife
Nothing about us like man and wife
She said my marriage brought this feeling
And afterwards life would be more appealing

There was a silent understanding
As I stood on my life's last landing
That if the change didn't end the urge
I could end the pain, She'd handle the dirge

She knows just how hard I tried
And wouldn't blame me if I died
As long as I made a real attempt
To leave the author of my self-contempt

And so at last, I took the leap
And broke the promise I meant to keep
Though in my mind there is no doubt
More than me, she wanted out

So here I am, alone at last
Facing fear and fading fast
My one last try, my final hope
Leading me fast to the loop of rope

Why some of them feel a fascination
For life despite the consternation
Is a thing I'll never understand
As I forever stand on shifting sand

Not for me are things ever certain
Indecision and doubt ring down my curtain
As I perform poorly on life's center stage
Quiet projection masks my inner rage

After all these years, I've come to know
The soul dies slowly from blow after blow
The urge to die rises surely up
As the constant critic fills your cup

As you quietly struggle to set yourself free
You turn into things you don't want to be
Until finally you simply begin to implode
From the forces outside you, the weight of your load

Thus have I arrived at this lonely place
Room for but one in this tiny space
The decision haunts me all the time
The answer's found within this rhyme

The End Game

I guess it's time to take a chance
And excuse myself from this painful dance
Efforts spent can't be recouped
Hard to accept that you've been duped

There was a time so long ago
When I could trust the things I knew
But it's clear to me now I didn't know
That love would leave and we'd be through

For love to leave is nothing new
But as long as mine for her still grew
I couldn't understand what I started to see
At the same time she was pulling away from me

Even as I try to make up my mind
And decide if I'm right or if I've been blind
I take a call from the answering machine
It's a call from a lawyer, now the break must be clean

Whimsey

Joe Smith

Me and My Eyes

Three of us stayed home today
Me, myself, and I
And all of us will swear to it
If one of us should lie

You'd think with all this company
We'd want a little time
To be alone all by ourselves
To try our hand at rhyme

But that's not why we feigned today
An illness to stay home
We have a need to keep at bay
The fear that in our heart does roam

Searching for a friend, you see
We've only just begun
But the way things have turned out so far
We might as well be done

But maybe we had something else
Upon our devious mind
Maybe what we all looked for
Missed us because we're blind

Maybe 'twas in front of us
Before our common I's
A you that would our heart capsize
And save us from our lies

A you that would always see
The forest and the trees
A you that truly could compete
With me and all my I's

Beauregard's Kitchen

Ma name is Beauregard
And I don't work too hard
Keep ma oven very clean
She's a lean clean machine

Sometimes I use a little pepper
Sometimes I use a little salt
Sometimes the food tastes all right
Other times, it ain't my fault

Some says ma kitchen's messy
Some says ma kitchen's quaint
Some folks like my cookin'
Some says I can cook, others says I cain't

Been awhile since I been sick
Been some time since I was blue
But if I give a thought real quick
Been awhile since I ate ma cookin', too

Yeah, they calls me Beauregard
Don't use no oil; cook with lard
Ma griddle slippery as a weasel
Ma flap jacks like a paintin' on an easel

Other night I baked a tater
Ate part; saved the rest for later
Mashed it up with a big metal spoon
Eat them spuds, too, you bet, real soon

Ain't the last you've heard from Beauregard
Ya can spell my name if ya tries real hard
But ya cain't find what I cook
By lookin' in ya ma's cookbook

Joe Smith

'Cause she don't soak her Lima beans
With dirty socks in her soup tureen
And she don't shuck her oysters raw
In her shoo fly pie with a crawdad paw

No she don't use no chicken beak
Or eye of newt laced with leek
And she don't pour a shot o' rye
Before she makes her mincemeat pie

Ya momma don't cook like Beauregard
'Cause she ain't had no true regard
For the cul'nary methods tried and true
That bring ma delicious treats to you

Alice's Mirror Part One

Through the magic looking glass
Alice thought she saw an ass
Wasn't I surprised to see
The ass she saw was really me?

Alice's Mirror Part Two

Into the magic looking glass
Alice saw she was an ass
The doctor gave her brand new glasses
Now she sees the other asses

The Fisherman

Sitting on a sunny beach
So much, it seems, is out of reach
Within this private world I've made
All things come to those who wade

Miscellaneous

Joe Smith

Morning Ride

Ride a cold morning
Your soul to win
Know what you're after
Before you go in

Ride a cold morning
And wait for the sun
To warm you up gently
Half into your run

Ride a cold morning
On fire belching steel
As dawn's visions greet you
Your mind starts to reel

Ride a cold morning
As the engine roars
Peace elsewhere for others
You have found yours

Ride a cold morning
All bundled up close
"Too cold" say some
But you need your dose

Ride a cold morning
On into the sun
Take images with you
When your ride is done

The View From The Mountain Top

I rode a cold morning to get here today
The morning's breath cold and the sky was all gray
It's been a long time since I've written you last
Thoughts for the future have grown from the past

I come to see you 'cause you never change
My thoughts, hopes, and feelings I try to arrange
There's nothing here I'm trying to construct
I'm merely here so I don't self-destruct

I'm wondering now if his mother can reach him
By leaving his love out, what's she trying to teach him?
The loss of my home and my one place to be
Is one other wonder that's worrying me

And what of religion that burns bright and fades,
Will I ever know it and find it in spades?
As I come here to sit on the edge of your brow
Saddened but soulful is how I feel now

A search for connection is harder I know
When the number of searchers around starts to grow
Lost in a forest of such diverse lives
I try to swim but my temperament dives.

I live my life in a chemical haze
But living without it leaves me in a daze
The dark days in number outlast the few
That I feel when I take time and spend it with you

All that I worked for seems now to be gone
But here with your nature I feel I belong
I load up my cycle with paper and pen
My hopes in my saddlebags, I come again

What do you know that I need to learn?
What do you give me that softens the yearn?
The breeze through the trees is conversation enough
But once I leave you the talking gets tough

The answer is somewhere here close at hand
But to finally hold it I must take a stand
I must move away from the fear and frustration
And find me some peace here of your creation

As long as I sit here and take in your view
I'm glad that you'll share, just me and you
And what of the children that come after me
Will they ever come here and see what I see?

I listened to her and have found things that I like
I found myself new friends, I bought me the bike
Each of these choices came at some cost
I made most too late, now I feel all is lost

Thank you for listening, my ancient friend
I leave you now but will come back again
For both our sakes I hope I will bring
A bag of hope and a reason to sing

But 'til then there's a strange irony I see
You can save me or kill me, either way I'll be free

Echo

I hear your voice
Dear Daddy still
Not what I want
But what you will

There's no one else
I've truly trusted
To know what's right
And well adjusted

Every time I start to think
Your voice comes booming through
And even if I don't concur
I take your point of view

With troubled but single personality
I muddle through each day
Still your voice lends duality
To all I do and say

I wonder just what might have been
If I had had the choice
To listen to or no ear lend
To the sound of your tired voice

Yes, wonder just what might have been
If you hadn't been my father
Could I to you have been a friend?
Or would you even bother?

Each time I take my pen in hand
To try to write what's true
I know there's nothing quite as grand
As what your hands could do

I measure each and every man
Against the mark you made
And I know that I never can
Roll down the tracks you laid

As I sit here on Christmas Eve
I cannot help but wonder
About the voice that I will leave
Will it cause them to blunder?

Or will I have a voice at all,
A whisper, SHOUT, or scream
To lead my children down the hall
Away from all that's mean?

I love you, Dad, don't take offense
But this to me is clear
A voice that keeps them on the fence
Is what I truly fear

I'd rather in the end they know
That one voice is all they need
Secure in knowing they should go
Where their own voices lead

Winging It On The Web

Working on the World Wide Web
Feeling all my confidence ebb
Trying then to stem the tide
Lack of experience my only guide

I spent last night in isolation
Causing me a great vexation
Resulting in some consternation
Ending up in full frustration
Much ado and aggravation
Now I need severe sedation

Dealing with some unknown forces
I know I should have had some courses
Guided by defaults that "Help" endorses
Better luck to bet on horses
My lack of mastery this reinforces

Instructions that seem pedantic
Push me through some odd antics
Can't relax, I grow frantic
My issues loom towards gigantic
Problems based on some semantics

Losing files I fully fear
All the words I hold so dear
Re-formatting's surely near
Passwords, it seems, are on my mind
Search for them until I'm blind
Without them I'm in a bind

Joe Smith

In Box

I'm waiting on an email
One may never come
I got one yesterday
Today I didn't get one

I sit and stare at the screen
In hopes I can conjure
A message to be seen
An in-box empty, I ponder

I wonder about my contacts
Are they delaying for lack of syntax?
Are they checking their vocabulary?
In fear of the language constabulary?

I wish they would arrange some bits
This waiting here, it gives me fits
A line in my in-box I'd like to see
A note or letter sent to me

Hoping for some inspiration
To leaven all this expectation
Fearing waves of sheer rejection
Causing this lack of some connection

I've waited long enough I think
But I don't want to cause a stink
I'm hoping for a short reply
I hope it comes before I die

He's Back

A friend of mine came back today
There's not much chance that he will stay
He's the one, the doltish dope
Who hasn't given up all hope

I read through the pages of Robert Frost
To find a feel at any cost
And just when I thought I was lost
He found me comfort there

I started off with *Mending Wall*
Familiar feelings there would call
I worked my way through *Witness Tree*
But I found nothing there for me

I plopped the pages and let them land
I found in the *Death of the Hired Hand*
That Mary found in Silas something grand
That Warren couldn't see

He pointed to a life worth less
No value there was my guess
But he and Mary said to me
There's hope in struggle, if you let it be

No victories won, no worlds to conquer
Left me cold and with a hunger
For something more than I can plan
To make of me a better man

But lying there between the lines
Covered in dust and settled in fines
He found a gem 'mongst all the rest
To struggle less sometimes is best

Silas went where he had to go
His brother's home would lay him low
He went back to a place he knew
Where no one's expectations grew

Mary saw in her compassion
We lead our lives in our own fashion
Some are meant for deeds so great
While others only live and wait

It wasn't that Silas won the prize
As death comes on our future dies
Not what he'd done before he died
It simply was that he had tried

He held his poem in front of me
Knowing that I'd finally see
That even if things don't work out
There's value in life beyond a doubt

Our progress toward our inner goal
Can be arrested as a whole
If the weight of all in our rucksack
Keeps each of us from going back

We need to know where we belong
To sing our part in life's long song
It's only when we let it be
That the best in us can be set free

I hope that he can stay awhile
And keep me from the Black Dog's trial
Maybe even bring a smile
To me on Christmas day

Complementary Universe

There is another universe
That parallels our own
And some of us that live in this
Call the other home

Within that other universe
The rules are much more sane
Everyone who lives in there
Knows everyone by name

There isn't any meanness there
No jealousy nor strife
Nothing here that can compare
With that better life

Confusion is a rarity
Within that other realm
What you get is what you see
We take turns at the helm

I choose at times to leave this world
And drift into my other
Especially when insults are hurled
And strike me or my brother

For in this world of parallels
Unlike my common home
There simply are no empty wells
No one is left alone

There simply are no "have to do s"
And no "there might have been s"
No film for the black and blues
Behind the camera's lens

<u>Joe Smith</u>

When transported to my other home
I'm always glad to see
That unlike this my earthly home
There is a place for me

Passage to this other world
Cannot be got for free
Three tickets should be held in hand
Music, books and poetry

There are of course some other ways
To slip across the void
It takes some time, but patience pays
Through reels of celluloid

Of all the ways, one's always sure
But real patience is required
By meditation slow but sure
This other world's acquired

Nature's still another way
For anyone to pass
Oh what a pleasant price to pay
To turn the looking glass

Passage can be also had
Through the artist's touch
But canvas sails can drive us mad
If oils touch us too much

But if the picture causes us
To see what isn't there
We're paid back in wanderlust
And fly off through the air

91

And when I make a short sojourn
To this place I write about
I know that I must soon return
Or else I'll be turned out

The time I spend in this other place
Is time well spent it's true
My passport stamp is on my face
It lasts a day or two

The benefit of traveling to
This ethereal oasis
Is found each time the songbirds sing
It gives my life some basis

If denied the benefit
Of passing back again
I'd perish from the lack of it
I'd die or be let in

I often wish that I could stay
And never more return
If I could only find a way
I'd never have to yearn

Cause in that world I'd be set free
From the pain of my reality
I'd be what I want to be
There's nothing there to limit me

No goodbyes to sear my soul
Loves lost come back and make me whole
Friends that here I've lost forever
Come to me there, we stay together

I'd sit and talk to my lost brother
Say things I wish I'd said
We'd laugh and joke and hold each other
Cause there he isn't dead

       And all the things I've never had
       Are there for me to gather
       I'd stop the pain of going mad
       Or rest there if I'd rather

    I'd have no need for blind ambition
    Those goals I cannot see
    I'd feel the comfort of true contrition
    I'd see inside of me

As much as I would like to stay
The landlord sends me on my way
He knows that I'll come back one day
When I have the strength to pay

Covid 19

A disease, it would seem, to be a strange topic
But avoiding it now seems somewhat myopic
To think it will end soon is such a delusion
Living life like we like is just an illusion

There's no doubt, it's changed our lives
While many have died, the virus thrives
We've all made changes to accommodate it
But so far there's no means to eradicate it

We hide behind masks, selves and friends to protect
But some of us feel this is a step to reject
A vaccine, it seems, is seen as the cure
We need one soon, that is for sure

Until things change then, we live in "New Normal"
Some changes casual and some of them formal
Funerals we hold which no mourners attend
All of us pray that this madness will end

No reunion, no parade, and no birthday party
It excludes no one, not the hale and the hardy
Though it's hardest on those found in assisted care
It spreads like wildfire the more that they share

As the pandemic proceeds families are split
People are frightened because of it
Statistics are gathered all in row
While the cases and deaths continue to grow

There was good news today about a new vaccine
Though there's tests to perform, the results to be seen
It seems, then, that we'll just have to wait
For this scourge that we're facing to finally abate

About the Author

Joseph "Joe" Smith was born in Louisville, Kentucky, in 1952, the fifth of ten children. He studied business management at the University of Louisville where he graduated with high honors in 1978.

Simultaneously, Joe worked in the plastics industry. He continued his work in this industry for another 34 years in various managerial positions in different locations throughout the United States.

Joe currently resides in a Senior Living Community in Chattanooga, Tennessee. He has two adult children who live in the greater Chattanooga area.

Poetry had long been an interest of Joe's, and during a protracted hospital stay in 1995, he began to write. His subject matter is widely varied and includes topics such as romance, psychology, and whimsy.

For many years, Joe has lived with bi-polar disorder – thus, the title of this compilation of his poems – *Life Between the Poles*.

Niagara Solid and Myriad Pro on LSI creme white
Type and Design by Karen Paul Stone